WHALES &
DOLPHINS

EXPLORER BOOKS

WHALES & DOLPHINS

by
Della Rowland

Published by The Trumpet Club
666 Fifth Avenue, New York, New York 10103

ISBN: 0-440-84351-0

Printed in the United States of America
September 1991

10 9 8 7 6 5 4 3 2 1
CW

PHOTOGRAPH CREDITS

p. 25: top, © A. W. Ambler from National Audubon Society/Photo Researchers,
Inc.; *bottom,* © Jen and Des Bartlett/Photo Researchers, Inc. *p. 26: top,* © Jen
and Des Bartlett/Photo Researchers, Inc.; *bottom,* © Ron Curbow from National
Audubon Society/Photo Researchers, Inc. *p. 27:* © Fred Bruemmer from
National Audubon Society/Photo Researchers, Inc. *p. 28: top,* Marineland of
Florida/Photo Researchers, Inc.; *bottom,* Jen and Des Bartlett/Photo Researchers,
Inc. *p. 29:* Franz Lazi/Photo Researchers, Inc. *p. 30:* © Francois Gohier/Photo
Researchers, Inc. *p. 31: top,* © James D. Watt/Animals Animals; *bottom,* Copy-
right 1989, Comstock/Russ Kinne. *p. 32: top,* © R. Llewellyn/Superstock; *bottom,*
© Dan Lloyd Taylor.

Cover: © Francois Gohier/Photo Researchers, Inc.

to baby Jackson Lloyd Taylor

Contents

1	Whales Today	1
2	What Is a Whale?	7
3	Whale Babies	15
4	Baleen Whales	22
5	Toothed Whales	38
6	The Smallest Whales	44

1

Whales Today

There are about eighty different *species*, or kinds, of whales. They are found in oceans all over the world—and some dolphins even live in rivers, too. Did you know that dolphins and porpoises are whales? They are the smallest whales.

Whales are truly marvelous creatures. For one thing, some species of whales are the largest animals ever to live on Earth. They are even larger than the dinosaurs were! And next to humans, whales are probably the most intelligent animals. What's more, they can see with their ears and communicate with other whales thousands of miles away.

But today whales need our help. Can you imagine the world without these awesome creatures? It could happen. Many species of whales are *endangered*. That means they are in danger of disappearing, or becoming *extinct*, like the dinosaurs. If whales become extinct, people won't be able to

1

bring them back! But we can do something now to help keep the whales alive. Here's how people are trying to help one whale named Humphrey.

Humphrey the Humpback Whale

In the fall of 1985, a *humpback* whale did something strange. He swam from the Pacific Ocean into California's San Francisco Bay. From there, the whale traveled 53 miles up the Sacramento River. Finally he came to a stop. *Marine biologists*, or scientists who study sea life, came from all over North America to study the odd behavior of this humpback whale. They named the whale Humphrey. Why would a huge whale leave his ocean home and travel into shallow waters? Nobody knew why. Scientists tried to scare Humphrey back down the river by making loud noises. They banged on pipes underwater, exploded small bombs, and gunned the motor of their boat. Nothing worked.

After 25 days, Humphrey's skin began to peel because he had been in fresh water too long. He was used to living in the Pacific Ocean, in salt water. If he stayed in the river much longer, he would die. Finally Dr. Louis Herman, an expert on whale communication, came up with a plan. He sent the scientists recordings he had made of the sounds humpbacks make when they are feeding.

The researchers boarded a boat with an underwater loudspeaker called a *hydrophone*. When they were about ½ mile away from Humphrey, they began playing the recordings. As soon as Humphrey heard the whale sounds, he froze, and then charged toward the boat.

The surprised researchers barely had time to get their boat in gear and head downstream! Humphrey followed the boat and the sounds for 7 hours—all the way down the river and back out into the Pacific Ocean. Humphrey was home free!

For years Humphrey was sighted many times swimming in the ocean. (Humpback whales can be identified by the shape of their tails, or *flukes*, and by the markings on their bodies.) Then, in October 1990, he swam into San Francisco Bay again! This time he swam right up onshore and got *stranded*, or stuck in the mud. And once again, he was rescued by concerned wildlife experts.

No one knows for sure why Humphrey keeps swimming into dangerous areas. But some scientists believe that he may not realize that he's heading into shallow waters. Polluted water, or bacteria, may have damaged his *echolocation* system—the way that whales "see" with sound waves. (You'll learn more about echolocation later in this book.) Whatever happened to Humphrey, it's clear that he needs human help! And so do other whales.

Whales in Trouble

There are only about 10,000 humpback whales left in the entire world. Not long ago there were about 115,000—almost twelve times as many! Ten thousand may sound like a large number of whales, but it isn't. The humpbacks that are left may not be able to reproduce quickly enough to keep the species from dying out. Pollution is killing many humpbacks and other kinds of whales. Whales are also being killed by whalers—people who hunt whales.

People have hunted whales for hundreds of years. Until recently, whale products were an important part of people's lives. Two hundred years ago, before we had electricity, whale oil was burned in lamps. Plastic hadn't been invented yet, and people used tough, springy whalebone to make springs for horse-drawn carriages, corsets, umbrellas, whip handles, fishing rods, nets, and brushes.

Today we have electricity and plastic, but the whale is still being hunted. Whale oil is used to grease expensive machinery. It is also used to make paint, varnish, ink, soap, margarine, and crayons. Whalebone is made into piano keys and other products. And whale meat is turned into fertilizer and pet food.

Several of the larger whales are endangered because of hunting. The gentle giants of the sea don't have a chance against modern hunting equipment. Whaling boats with powerful engines can catch even the swift blue whale.

The chart on page 5 tells how many whales existed before whaling and how many were left in 1989. It is very hard to count whales in the ocean, so these numbers are only an estimate.

Dolphins, the smallest whales, are in grave danger from fishing companies. Tuna fishermen watch for dolphins in order to locate the prized yellowfin tuna. For some reason, the tuna swim underneath

WHALES THEN AND NOW

WHALE	BEFORE WHALING	1989
Fin	548,000	120,000
Sei	256,000	54,000
Blue	228,000	14,000
Humpback	115,000	10,000
Bowhead	30,000	7,800
Southern Right	100,000	3,000
Northern Right	?	1,000

the dolphins. Some scientists think they do this to feed on the fish that the dolphins hunt. Fishermen surround the tuna with nets called *purse seines* (purs saynz). Dolphins swimming above the tuna are dragged underwater by the nets. Every year about 100,000 dolphins drown this way.

Conservation groups tried to make tuna companies stop killing dolphins, by forming a national *boycott.* These groups joined together and agreed not to buy products made by tuna companies until they stopped catching dolphins. Some companies, like Starkist, did stop.

Plastic drift nets are causing trouble for dolphins, too. Fishing companies stretch out miles of drift nets at night and haul them in each morning. These nets are so thin that the dolphin's keen echolocation cannot sense them. Dolphins and other air-breathing creatures—even seabirds—become caught in these nets and drown.

Garbage and pollution are also killing dolphins and whales. They can die from eating plastic thrown into the ocean. Toxic waste, or poisons, in the oceans killed about 8,000 dolphins and 15 humpbacks in

1987. And several *gray* whales died when an Exxon Oil Company ship, the *Valdez*, spilled 11 million gallons of oil into the waters near Alaska.

Protecting the Whales

Today many countries, including the United States, make laws to protect whales. The U.S. Marine Mammal Protection Act of 1972 states that no one may harm or disturb these animals in U.S. waters. Because of this law, fishermen must release dolphins and porpoises that get caught in their nets.

So many species of whales are now endangered, that the International Whaling Commission banned whaling in 1985. But some countries, such as Japan, Norway, and the Soviet Union, still hunt whales. Organizations such as Greenpeace are fighting hard to stop them. Greenpeace workers in small boats stop in front of large whaling ships. They risk their lives to end the slaughter of whales.

Why do people risk their lives to protect whales? And why is it important that we learn about them? In this book you'll find out why whales—from the huge blue whale to the tiny dolphin—are among the most fascinating creatures on Earth.

2

What Is a Whale?

Scientists call all whales *cetaceans* (see-TAY-shuns). However, there are actually two groups of whales—those with teeth and those without teeth. Teeth make a difference in the way a whale catches its food.

Toothed whales are called *Odontoceti* (o-DON-tuh-see-tee). *Odonto* means "tooth" and *ceti* means "whales." The other group of whales has baleen instead of teeth. *Baleen* is another word for "whalebone," which people used before plastic was invented. Baleen whales are called *Mysticeti* (MISS-tuh-see-tee). *Mysti* means "mustaches." Whales with baleen look as if they have mustaches. Later in this book you'll discover how baleen and teeth help a whale catch its food. But first you'll find out exactly what a whale is.

Is a Whale a Fish?

A whale spends all of its time in the water. This

WHALE FAMILY CHART

ODONTOCETI	MYSTICETI
Sperm	Right
Beaked	Gray
Bottlenose	Rorquals: Blue,
Narwhals	Fin, Sei, Humpback,
Belugas	Bryde's, Minke
Ocean Dolphins	
(including Orcas	
and Pilot Whales)	
River Dolphins	
Porpoises	

means whales are fish, right? Wrong! A whale is a *mammal*, an air-breathing creature just like you. A whale is a marine, or sea, mammal. Other marine mammals include seals, sea lions, sea otters, walruses, and manatees.

Mammals are warm-blooded animals, like dogs, cats, cows, and horses. Whales and other mammals have a body temperature that stays the same no matter how cold or hot the air or water becomes. A fish is cold-blooded. Its body temperature changes so that it is always the same as the water it swims in.

One big difference between mammals and fish is the way they have babies. Most mammal babies grow inside the mother until they are completely developed. After a mammal is born, its mother nurses it with milk. Mammal mothers stay with their babies and teach them how to take care of themselves. Whales give birth to living, fully developed babies that nurse. Most fish, however, never even see their babies. They lay their eggs and then swim away. After the eggs hatch, the fish babies are on their own. The babies don't need their mothers. They can find their own food right away and take care of themselves.

Mammals and fish also breathe differently. Mammals breathe oxygen with their lungs. Fish take in oxygen from the water through their gills. Whales come to the water's surface regularly in order to breathe air into their lungs.

A mammal usually has hair or fur on its body to help keep it warm, but a fish is covered with scales. At one time whales had fur, and some still have a few hairs. Now they have an extra-thick layer of fat to keep them warm. Instead of scales, they have thick, smooth skin. If you touched this skin, it would feel like soft rubber.

Scientists believe that the whale's closest relative on land may be the cow. Whale stomachs are like those of cows. In fact, the male of both animals is called a bull; the female is a cow; and the baby is a calf. Groups of whales are sometimes called herds, although they are usually called *pods*.

But even though whales are sea mammals, they haven't always lived in the water. Millions of years ago, whales walked on land!

Whales on Land

Before you start trying to figure out how a giant whale would look walking around on the beach—wait! Early whales didn't look much like the whales we know today. For one thing, they were much smaller. Scientists think they might have been about the size of a human being or smaller. They probably looked more like a dog, a rat, or maybe an otter. They had four legs and their bodies were covered with fur.

The oldest fossils of whales are about 50 million years old. These fossils have given us clues about what whales used to look like and how they moved about. But even without these fossils, we could learn a lot about early whales simply by examining whales today. Inside a whale's flipper, for example, there are finger bones—just like those of a human hand! And there is still a hip bone left over in the whale's skeleton. These bones show us that early whales had hands or paws and back legs.

An unborn baby whale looks something like an ancient whale. As they develop, they change and become whales as we know them today. Unborn whales have four tiny legs that disappear before they are born. At first the nostrils are on the front of the baby's face. But as the baby develops, the nostrils move up to the top of the head. They become an opening called a *blowhole.* A whale breathes through its blowhole the way you breathe through your nose.

Return to the Water

Why did the whales' ancestors leave the land and go to live in the sea? It might have had a lot to do with food. Scientists believe that early whales lived along the shores of oceans or rivers and ate fish they caught in the shallow water. When food became scarce, they began swimming farther out where there was more to eat.

Over the centuries, these first whales began to spend more and more time in the water. Their bodies then began to change, or *evolve,* to make it easier for them to live in water. This process took place very, very slowly. It took millions and millions of years for these land animals to change into sea creatures. Their bodies became longer and more bullet-shaped. This way, they were more streamlined for easier swimming. Over thousands of years, the whale's back legs gradually disappeared, and its front legs became flat, smooth *flippers.* Underwater, flippers are better for steering than legs and feet are because they are shaped like paddles.

Many species of whales developed a back fin called the *dorsal.* The dorsal fin helps the whale keep its balance. And the long, narrow tail became flat and wide. This kind of tail helps the whale move through the water faster, the way rubber flippers help divers swim. To move itself forward, a whale waves its tail—called a *fluke*—up and down.

On land, the whale's fur helped it stay warm and dry. But in the water, wet fur was cold and heavy. For this reason, fur eventually disappeared from the whale. All that's left of it now is a few bristles on the chins of some whales. Fur was replaced with *blubber,* a thick layer of fat under the skin. Depending upon the size of the whale, blubber can be anywhere from 2 inches to 2 feet thick! Blubber can keep a whale warm even in the freezing waters of

Antarctica. It is also a storehouse of food that the whale can live on when food becomes scarce.

Breathing in the Water

One part of the whale that *didn't* change was its lungs. The whale still had to breathe in oxygen from the air. Yet it also had to stay underwater long enough to find food. Breathing with lungs became easier as the whale's nostrils gradually moved from the front of its face up to the top of its head. When the whale needed to breathe, it didn't have to lift its heavy body out of the water. It could just poke the top of its head up above the surface.

As whales began to spend more and more time underwater, they became able to hold their breath for long periods of time. While they are diving, their heart rates slow down and their muscles use less oxygen. The blowholes close up tight so that no water can get inside. *Sperm* whales, the largest of the toothed whales, can hold their breath longer than any other kind of whale. They can stay underwater for 1½ hours!

When a whale finally comes up for air, it needs to breathe right away. It can exhale, or breathe out air, at a rate of 300 miles an hour! This burst of air looks like a spout of water shooting out of the blowhole. When a whale exhales, it is called *spouting*. This spout, called a whale's *blow,* is actually air that has become warm and moist from being held inside the whale's lungs. When the warm air hits the cooler air outside the whale's body, it turns into a steamy spout. The same thing happens when you exhale in cold weather. Your warm breath makes fog in the cold air!

Different whales have different-shaped spouts. Many experts can tell whales apart just by seeing their spouts. The shape of the spout is partly determined by how many blowholes a whale has—one or two. Toothed whales have one blowhole, while baleen whales have two. *Right* whales have two blowholes that form a V-shaped spout. The *blue* whale also has two blowholes, but its spout is pear-shaped. A sperm whale has one blowhole far to the left side of its huge head. Its 12-foot spout blows to one side rather than straight up.

How Whales Got So Big

Whales weren't always as large as they are today. It took millions of years for them to evolve into giants. Some whales are so large that they are called the *great whales*. The great whales include the toothed *sperm* and all the baleen whales except the *minke*—the *blue*, the *fin*, the *right*, the *sei* (say), the *humpback*, the *gray*, and the *Bryde's*.

The blue whale is the largest of the great whales. In fact, it is the largest creature that ever lived on Earth. It can grow to be 100 feet long—as long as eight cars lined up end to end. It is twice as long as the largest dinosaur, the brontosaurus. It weighs nearly 200 tons, or 400,000 pounds—as heavy as thirty elephants! Its tongue alone weighs as much as one elephant does!

Scientists think that a large food supply is one of the reasons these whales grew so big. The more the whales ate, the bigger they became. One giant blue whale can eat 16,000 pounds of food every day.

But the main reason whales were able to keep growing is that they lived in the water. On land, their size was limited by how much weight their legs could carry. The more an animal weighs, the bigger its leg bones must be in order to carry the weight. In order to walk, a blue whale would need legs that were four times thicker than those of the largest dinosaur. This would make the leg bone too heavy for the whale to lift.

A whale doesn't need legs to hold it up, however. Its enormous weight is supported by water. Great whales are swift, mighty creatures in the sea, but they are helpless on land. A stranded whale is able to live for several days. But breathing becomes more and more difficult without water to support its body. Water is also necessary to protect the whale from drying out in the sun. The sooner the tide comes in to carry the beached whale back out to sea, the better!

3

Whale Babies

By watching small whales in aquariums, scientists learn about the way whales mate, give birth, and raise their young. It isn't as easy to watch the great whales because they swim all over the huge, deep ocean. Most of them have never been seen mating or giving birth.

Mating Rituals

Most whales have their babies in warm waters. During the summer they feed in the cold waters near the North and South Poles. When the polar waters freeze over in winter, the whales migrate to warm waters to give birth. The babies need to begin life in warm waters. They don't have much blubber when they are born. Without this protective fat, they could die in the freezing, arctic waters.

Whales often mate in the warm waters, too. Males usually try to attract females by showing off.

Some wave their flukes. Others leap up into the air, or *breach*, over and over again. The male *narwhal* waves its 10-foot-long spiral tusk. Humpbacks sing to their mates. Male sperm whales have bloody fights over females, ramming and breaking each other's jaws.

Once they've chosen mates, whales spend time getting to know each other. They swim side by side and roll over and leap together. They nuzzle and nibble each other and stroke each other with their flippers. After they mate, a tiny egg inside the female begins to develop into a big baby.

The time it takes for a mammal baby to develop inside its mother is called the *gestation period.* Since whales are such huge creatures, you'd think it would take a long time for a baby whale to develop. But a large whale baby develops almost as quickly as human babies do.

It takes 9 months for the average human baby to grow to 7 or 8 pounds. But it takes only 11 months for the egg of a blue whale to grow into a baby that is 25 feet long and weighs 15,000 pounds! The baby blue whale is the biggest baby in the world. The longest gestation period among whales is 16 months for sperm whales. The shortest is 8 months for porpoises. For most whales, the gestation period is between 10 and 12 months.

Underwater Birth

You and most other mammals are usually born headfirst. This allows you to breathe right away even though the rest of your body hasn't come out into the air yet. But you are born on land with air all around you. Whales are born underwater, so it makes sense for them to come out tailfirst. If a whale came out headfirst, water might enter its blowhole. It would drown before it was born.

As soon as a baby whale is born, it swims to the surface. If it needs help, its mother or another cow is right under it, pushing it upward. The baby's first lesson is how to breathe. Its second lesson is how to nurse underwater.

A baby whale has to nurse quickly, since it has to surface often in order to breathe. When it gets hungry, the baby places its mouth over its mother's nipple. The mother then squeezes the strong muscles in her milk glands and squirts milk into her baby's mouth. This method of feeding allows the calf to eat in between breaths! Whale babies feed about 40 times a day.

Whale milk is very rich. It is about 50 percent fat. A cow's milk is only about 4 percent fat. People who have had whale milk say it tastes like a mixture of milk of magnesia, fish, liver, and castor oil. That may not sound very appealing to you, but to a whale baby it's delicious.

This rich, fatty milk helps whale babies gain up to 200 pounds a day—about the weight of four children! They're able to gain this much weight by drinking up to 130 gallons of milk a day. Most baby whales nurse for about 6 months to 2 years. But male sperm whales may take an occasional gulp of milk until they are 10 years old!

Learning To Talk

A baby whale learns to "talk" just as you did when you were an infant. The adults teach each new baby how to make sounds that will help it take care of itself. Whales make sounds that scientists believe are different signals for *food, mother, play,* and *danger.* Young whales make special whistles and squeaks which their parents respond to.

Whales "talk" to let one another know where they are and where food is. They warn one another if danger is near. They chatter back and forth, and call out to other pods miles away. The sounds a fin whale makes can be heard 2,000 miles away. This means that two fin whales can keep in touch with each other even though they're on opposite sides of the Pacific Ocean.

Unlike you, whales have no vocal cords with which to make sounds. Instead, the sounds are vibrations that sound like creaking doors, whistles, squeaks, or clicks. Some of the sounds are too high for the human ear to hear. Dolphins and other small whales whine and squeal and make squeaks, chirps, and clicks. Large whales tend to make low moans, groans, and grunts.

Whales use these sounds to communicate with each other. Amazingly, they also use sound to "see." As a whale travels through the water, it makes short bursts of sound through its blowhole. When these sound waves hit an object, such as a fish, boat, rock, or sandbar, they bounce back to the whale's ears like an echo. From this echo, whales can tell where something is and how big it is. The closer an object is, the quicker the echo comes back. In this way, whales use sound echoes to "see." This way of locating things is called *echolocation* (ek-oh-lo-KAY-shun). Submarines use sound, or *sonar*, waves in the same way.

Sound travels very fast in water—about 1 mile per second. If a school of fish is 1 mile away, a whale can "see" it within 2 seconds. It takes 1 second for the sound to reach the fish and 1 second for it to return to the whale.

Whales need to use echolocation to "see." First of all, their eyes are set far back on either side of their head. This makes it difficult for them to see what's in front of them. What's more, there isn't enough light in the deep ocean for whales to be able to rely on their vision.

It's possible that whales can even "hear" what an object looks like. Their ears may send signals that turn into pictures in their brains, just as your eyes send picture signals to your brain. Using echolocation, a mother dolphin can spot a gas bubble inside her baby's stomach. She can then burp her baby by bumping it in just the right place.

Toothed whale babies must learn "echolocation manners." Just like human babies, they are taught that it is rude to point. That is, they cannot point their head toward another whale. If they do, they might "zap" that whale with their echolocation sounds. These sounds are called the whale's *spray*. A toothed whale's spray is very strong. It can actually stun living things in its path. Scientists have watched baby dolphins in tanks as they learn to swim in pods. At first the babies swim every which way. Often they point toward their mother and she has to move. But they soon learn to behave themselves.

Sometimes a whale's echolocation doesn't work and it can become stranded on land. When it starts crying for help, other whales might swim to its rescue and become stranded, too. If whales are hurt or separated from their pod, they will send out the same signal over and over again until other whales come. A boater once watched about twenty-five female sperm whales come from miles around—just to answer the "help" call of one injured calf!

Growing Up

While a baby is nursing, it stays close to its mother for protection, food, and education. It usually rides right beneath its mother's belly or tail, or the mother and baby swim flipper to flipper.

Whale *aunts* often help baby-sit while the mother goes off to feed. The aunt fusses over the baby as if it were her own. If there is any danger, she will act as a guard while the mother and baby escape to safety. An aunt will even adopt a calf if its mother dies.

Whale mothers like to play with their babies. Gray whales will swim underneath their babies, then shoot air out of their blowholes. The whirl of bubbles sends the little whales spinning. Mother grays also like to bounce their young ones up and down with their noses. They've even been seen hugging their babies with their flippers. Adult sperm whales touch their young with their jaws, as if they were kissing them.

Whale calves behave just like human children. They are sometimes mischievous or annoying. For some reason, they enjoy crawling up on their mother's back when she's trying to nap. Or they may wander off. Baby whales don't always obey their mothers, who sometimes run out of patience. One dolphin-style punishment is to hold a little one underwater for a few seconds.

Taking care of a baby whale is a big job. Luckily whales have one baby at a time, and they give birth only about every 2 to 4 years. This way, a whale mother has plenty of time to help her baby prepare to live on its own. When a baby is ready to eat food, it begins to spend less time with its mother. It soon learns how to catch its own food and take care of itself. When the calf is about 4 to 6 years old, it will be an adult that can have babies of its own.

4

Baleen Whales

Baleen is called whalebone, but it isn't bone at all. It's made up of keratin, the same material that's found in your fingernails. Long, thin blades, or plates, of baleen grow down from the whale's upper jaw. These plates are shaped like triangles. Each plate is bristly at the bottom.

A baleen whale has hundreds of these plates hanging down from each side of its mouth. Each plate can be as tall as a doorway! Even though baleen plates are a little stiff, they are not used like teeth to bite, tear, or chew. A simple way to explain how baleen whales eat is to describe *what* they eat.

The Biggest Eat the Smallest

What can a whale with a mouthful of bristles eat? The answer is something small. These whales eat *krill*. Krill are orange creatures about 2 inches

22

long that look like shrimp. Krill feed on plants that are so small they can only be seen through a microscope. These plants are green, jelly-like blobs that are shaped like circles, squares, and stars. The krill and tiny plants float in the ocean like an orange cloud. This animal and plant mixture is called *plankton.*

When a hungry baleen whale wants to eat, it simply swims through the ocean, taking in great mouthfuls of plankton and water. Then it forces the water back out through the spaces in its baleen. The krill are trapped in the baleen's hairy bristles inside the whale's mouth. All the whale has to do is sweep the krill down its throat with its tongue. This meal doesn't try to swim away, as a fish or a squid would. Since plankton floats near the surface, the whales don't even have to dive for their dinner. In addition, plankton is plentiful, so baleen whales can eat huge helpings at every meal.

Big Blue

The biggest baleen whale—and the biggest animal in the world—is the blue whale. As you might guess from its name, the blue whale is a dark blue flecked with white. A full-grown blue would stretch across an entire basketball court, with its tail covering the first few rows of seats. Its spout shoots up 20 feet into the air. Its heart is the size of a small car! And its eyes are as big as your entire head.

The blue whale weighs as much as 3,000 children

would weigh—about 150,000 pounds—and eats up to 16,000 pounds of krill each day. In order to eat that much, it has to be able to take big bites. That is no problem for a blue!

Under the blue whale's chin and belly there are between sixty and ninety grooves. These grooves look like stripes, but they are actually folds, or pleats, in the whale's throat. When the whale fills its mouth, the pleats unfold and its throat expands like a balloon. The throat expands until it's six times bigger than its normal size. This allows the whale to gulp hundreds of gallons of food. That's why scientists call these pleated whales *gulpers*.

The Beautiful Rorquals

The pleats in a blue whale's throat are what give the animal its family name, rorqual (ROAR-kwul). *Rorqual* is a Norwegian word that means "whale pleats" or "grooves." There are five other rorqual whales: the fin, the sei, the Bryde's, the minke, and the humpback.

There are no small rorquals. Even the runt of this family, the minke, is 30 feet long. The Bryde's whale, which is rarely seen, is about 42 feet long. The humpback and the sei are usually 60 feet long. And the fin whale can grow up to 80 feet long.

Long, slender, and streamlined, the rorquals move gracefully through the deep oceans. Their strong, sleek bodies are built for swift swimming. A blue whale can swim up to 30 miles per hour!

Pure white belugas live in chilly, arctic waters. They can bend their necks to face each other and can change the shape of their lips.

A fin whale inhales through its double blowhole.

Whales are often identified by the markings on their tails.
This is the fluke of a southern right whale.

The orca is truly a killer whale when hunting prey in the
ocean, but is gentle in captivity.

This narwhal is stranded on a Baffin Island beach. You can tell
it is a male by its 10-foot-long spiral tusk.

A bottlenose dolphin mother swims flipper to flipper with her baby.

Several dolphins swim together in the Sea of Cortez, off of Mexico.

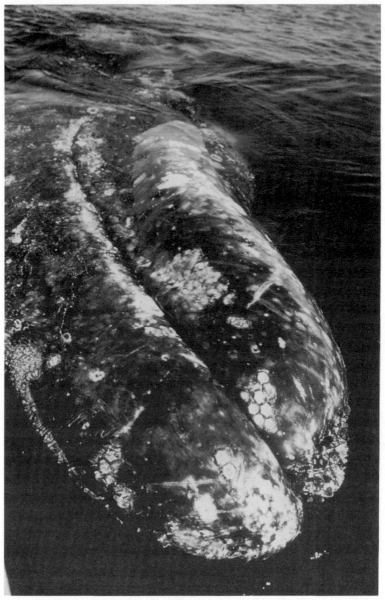

The head of this California gray whale is covered with lice
and barnacles.

Ahoy there! A spouting blue whale up ahead!

Two humpback whales in a double breach off the Hawaiian coast.

A narwhal swims with her 1-hour-old calf near Baffin Island.

Dolphins seem friendly because they always look as if they're smiling–but that's just the way their mouths are shaped.

Dolphins in captivity enjoy having their throats scratched by their trainers.

The Homely Humpback

Imagine that you are on a whale-watching boat in the ocean. As you look out over the water, you see a white spray shooting up. Just as your boat reaches the spot, a creature as big as a school bus leaps 30 feet out of the water! "It's a humpback!" shouts one of the crew members.

The whale flaps its long, ragged 16-foot flippers as if it were going to fly. For a second, its huge body seems to hang in midair. Then, with a graceful flip, this 50-ton giant turns a somersault and crashes back down. It hits the water with a thundering splash that shoots up 20 feet high. The last thing you see is the animal's tail waving before it smacks the water and disappears. The whale has just breached.

No one knows exactly why humpbacks and other whales breach. Because the splash is so big and so loud, they may be sending messages to other whales. Or they may be showing off for a whale with which they want to mate. Humpbacks have been seen breaching up to 40 times without stopping. (The humpback gets its name from the way it humps its back when it dives.)

Other rorqual whales are long, sleek, and smooth. But the humpback is rather stout and is covered with warts and knobby lumps. These knobs and bumps are actually lice and barnacles. One humpback may carry up to ½ ton of barnacles! Scientists think humpbacks may be trying to get rid of the lice and barnacles when they breach.

Humpbacks are different from other rorquals in that they eat small fish rather than plankton. They often catch their food in bubble nets. The whale swims in circles underneath a school of fish, blowing bubbles out of its blowholes. The frightened fish crowd together inside this "ring" of bubbles. To catch the trapped fish, all the humpback has to do is swim straight up with its mouth open.

Humpback whales are famous for their singing. Their songs have beginnings, endings, and parts that repeat, and they can last for a half hour. Many people have recorded the humpback's songs, and these recordings can be bought in some stores. The low, whistling squeaks and long, shrill wails of the humpback may sound sad or eerie to you.

When they get ready to sing, humpbacks take several deep breaths and dive. About 50 feet down, they screech to a halt and assume their favorite singing position—which is upside down! Hanging completely still in the water, the whales sing until they have to go up to the surface again to breathe.

Only male humpbacks sing, and they sing only during mating time—about 6 months out of the year. Researchers think they might be trying to attract females, or scare other males away from the females in the area. All the humpbacks in one area usually sing the same song. During the mating season, the song changes slowly. This means the humpbacks are listening carefully to all the other singers and are learning the song from one another. After mating in warmer waters, the humpbacks return to their polar feeding grounds. There they stop singing. But they remember the last song, and they begin the new mating season with it.

Did you know that the song of the humpback whale has been sent into space? In 1977, the spaceships *Voyager 1* and *Voyager 2* were launched into outer space. On board the ships was a recording called *The Sounds of Earth*. This recording included greetings in fifty-five different languages. One of the greetings was the song of a humpback whale!

Right Whales

The right whales got their name from old-time whalers because they were the "right" whales to hunt. The right's 60-foot body contained thousands of pounds of valuable baleen and blubber. These gentle giants swam slowly, so they were easy to catch. Best of all, they floated after they were killed.

Right whales belong to the baleen family, but they do not have pleated throats like the rorquals. However, eating is just as easy for them. Unlike the rorquals, the rights do not gulp. Instead, they swim slowly through the water with their mouths open. Their huge baleen plates filter plankton and krill out of the water. Every few minutes they close their mouths and swallow. This way of feeding is called *skimming*.

One of the first things you notice about a right whale is its baleen. It curves down over the whale's great arched mouth. When its mouth is open, the baleen is just about all you can see of the whale!

That's because the right whale's head takes up one-third of its entire body—and most of its head is its mouth!

There are three kinds of right whales. The Greenland whale is the largest—about 60 feet long. Its mouth is curved like a huge bow, which is how it got its other name, the bowhead whale. It has 800 baleen plates that can grow up to 14 feet long! When the whale wants to close its mouth, the blades fold up and fit into grooves inside the mouth.

Wayfaring Gray Whales

Instead of krill, gray whales eat crabs, clams, and small fish. These creatures live at the bottom of shallow waters. This may be the reason grays live close to shore rather than in the deep ocean where the rorquals and the rights swim.

Grays have about 300 baleen plates and 4 pleats beneath their mouths. Yet they don't gulp like the rorquals, or skim like the rights. They shovel. This is the only way they can get their favorite foods. To eat, a gray dives down to the ocean bottom. It rolls over onto its side and scoops a big helping of mud and sand up into its mouth. Then it rears upright, squirts out the muddy water, and swallows the food that's trapped in its baleen.

Gray whales are found only in the Pacific Ocean. Each year they travel about 8,000 miles—from the cold North Pole down to the warm Gulf of California, then back again. Since grays are not the fastest swimmers, it takes them about 3 months to make the entire trip.

The gray whale's migration is different from that of other whales. Amazingly, gray whales migrate to the same spot each winter. Animals that *migrate* move from one region to another with the change in seasons. They mate and have their babies in the warmer region. Every year the grays mate in the warm gulf waters, before they begin their migration to the north. Later in the year, they swim south again to have their babies. Baby grays begin life in the quiet lagoons of Baja California. In these safe, warm waters, the calves mature and grow a thick layer of blubber.

Returning to the same mating place year after year has helped the population of the gray whale to grow. They nearly died out twice because of whalers. At one time, there were only about 100 of them left. Now there are about 21,000. The gray whale is one of the few great whales whose numbers seem to be increasing.

5

Toothed Whales

There are sixty-six kinds of Odontoceti, or toothed whales. The strange thing about them is that they don't use their teeth to eat. At least, they don't chew their food—they swallow it whole! Odontoceti use their teeth mostly to *catch* their food.

All but three of the toothed whales are between 3 and 16 feet long. Baleen whales are from 30 to 100 feet long. Toothed whales may be smaller than baleen whales because they must work harder to catch their food. Toothed whales have to be fast swimmers in order to catch the fish and squid that they eat. Having a large body would slow them down. On the other hand, baleen whales don't have to use much energy to catch plankton. They simply swim through the oceans with their mouths open.

Battling Jaws

Unlike other toothed whales, a sperm whale

doesn't use its teeth for catching food. This whale doesn't even have a complete set of teeth until it is 30 or 40 years old! Even then it has only about twenty-five, and all of them are on its bottom jaw. So what does a sperm whale use its teeth for?

For one thing, males use their teeth to fight one another for females. Females and calves live in pods of twenty to fifty members called *harems*. During mating season, males fight one another for control of a harem. The male that wins will be able to mate with the females in that harem.

During these fierce battles, two males ram their huge heads together. They bite each other, tearing off hunks of flesh. They hold on to each other's jaws and wrestle. Finally, one gives up and swims away, but both whales are usually hurt. Male sperm whales are often seen with bloody wounds all over their heads, or with limp, broken jaws full of chipped teeth.

The sperm whale's favorite food is squid. These whales usually eat squid that are about 1 to 2 feet long. However, the larger males will hunt 50-foot giant squid! To find these huge sea monsters, the sperm whale will dive as deep as 2 miles and stay down for 1½ hours!

Giant squid are almost as long as the male sperm whales, which are 60 feet long and weigh 120,000 pounds. No one has ever seen these two giants battle, but here's what scientists believe happens. The sperm whale dives deep down into the ocean. It uses echolocation to find a giant squid in the inky black water. The whale stuns the squid with a spray of rapid-fire sound waves. It then grabs the squid's giant head in its jaws and tries to swallow it.

To keep from being swallowed, the squid wraps its long tentacles around the whale's head, and the two giants thrash around in the dark. The whale usually manages to swallow the squid. But the whale's head and jaw are left covered with large, round scars. They are made by the hard edges of the squid's powerful suckers.

The squid also leaves behind its hard beak, which the whale cannot digest. The whale's stomach or intestines form an oily blob around the beak called *ambergris.* Whalers used to hunt sperm whales because perfume companies paid a lot of money for ambergris. It was needed to make expensive perfumes. Back then, finding valuable ambergris in a whale was like discovering buried treasure.

The sperm whale's square head makes up one-third of its body and contains huge amounts of a clear, oily liquid. Long ago, whalers thought this liquid was the whale's sperm. They called the oil *spermaceti,* or seed of the whale. (And that's how the sperm whale got its name.) Before electric lights were invented, sperm whales were hunted for this oil. Outside the whale's warm body, the liquid cools into a solid white wax. Because this wax burned brightly without smoke, it was used to make fine candles. One sperm whale can produce as much as 15 tons of spermaceti!

Once there were about 2½ million sperm whales. Researchers now believe that there are only a few hundred thousand of them left. Since these divers spend so much time in deep water, however, it is hard to tell exactly how many there are.

The Unicorn and the Sea Canary

The narwhal whale has only two teeth. But the male's left front tooth grows through the upper lip until it is 10 feet long! Because of this one long tooth, the narwhal is also called the unicorn. No one has ever figured out just what the male narwhal does with its awesome spiral tusk. Most scientists believe it is used to attract females.

Narwhals look very much like beluga whales except for their teeth. Whereas narwhals have one huge tooth, belugas have about forty small ones. Narwhals are brown and spotted like a leopard, whereas belugas are pure white.

Narwhals and belugas are both plump with round heads that look like melons and faces that make them look as if they're smiling. They are small for whales—about 16 feet long. Both of them make their home in the arctic waters all year round.

Beluga whales were nicknamed "sea canaries" by British sailors because of their high-pitched chirps and whistles. These white whales trill, squeak, grunt, and clap their jaws together loudly. The sounds were so loud that the sailors could hear them inside their ships!

Belugas live in huge pods. Sometimes more than 10,000 of them travel together at one time! They use body language to communicate with other members of the pod. They can bend their necks so that they face one another. And they are the only whales that can change the shape of their lips.

Killer Whales

The *orca* is the second-largest toothed whale. Males can grow to 32 feet long and weigh 18,000 pounds. They have a dorsal fin that is 6 feet tall!

The orca is actually a type of dolphin. It is the largest member of the dolphin family, so large that it is called a whale. (The 20-foot-long pilot whale is also a member of the dolphin family. And it, too, is called a whale because of its enormous size.) An orca, like other dolphins, can be very playful and friendly. But this dolphin is also the most feared creature in the ocean. It isn't afraid of anything, including humans!

There are a number of reasons why orcas are so frightening. For one thing, they can reach speeds of 30 miles per hour. This makes it easy for them to chase and capture most sea creatures. Orcas can leap and turn quickly, too, so they can grab animals off the ice or the shore. In addition, they have fifty large, cone-shaped teeth that can snap a 700-pound seal in half. Even sharks fear this whale's bite!

Orcas are called killer whales because they are the only whales that eat other sea mammals. They eat penguins, seals, sea lions, and other whales. They also eat birds, and even sharks! But their main food is fish and squid. The orca is as beautiful as it is powerful. It looks as if someone painted large white designs on its shiny black body.

About fifty orcas live in a pod, which is very much like a tightly knit family. An orca spends its entire life in the same pod. Even after it has grown up, it remains very close to its mother. A pod takes care of sick or injured members. These small whales are very organized hunters, and they often work together to catch their prey. By hunting in a pack, orcas can even kill a huge blue whale!

Now that you know how fierce orcas are, would you believe that they make wonderful pets? A number of orcas live in sea aquariums, where they become as tame as their close relatives, the bottlenose dolphins. Orcas even swim in the same tank with these dolphins! In the open seas, orcas might eat bottlenose dolphins, but never in an aquarium. This is partly because the orcas in aquariums are kept well fed.

If you see an orca trying to swallow its trainer's arm, don't worry. The whale is only trying to get its tongue and throat stroked! Orcas love to be petted by their trainers and to spend time with people. They are very curious about humans. Trainers say that the orca's lack of fear makes it a better student than other dolphins. Other dolphins are more difficult to train and will hesitate during a trick because they are afraid. But an orca can be taught to jump completely out of the water—with its trainer sitting on its nose!

6

The Smallest Whales

The smallest toothed whales are the dolphins and the porpoises. Including the orca and the pilot whale, there are thirty-two kinds of oceanic dolphins, five kinds of river dolphins, and six kinds of porpoises! However, bottlenose dolphins are the ones with which people are most familiar. They are usually the star performers in aquariums. Flipper, the TV star, is a bottlenose dolphin.

Sometimes it's hard to tell dolphins and porpoises apart. The easiest way is to look at their snouts. Dolphins usually have pointed jaws that look something like a beak, whereas porpoises have blunt noses. Porpoises are also shorter and fatter than dolphins. They are about 3 to 6 feet long. Dolphins are 6 to 15 feet long. The stout porpoises are slow swimmers, while the sleek dolphins are much more energetic. Another difference between the two animals is the shape of their teeth. Dolphins have cone-shaped teeth. Porpoises have teeth that look more like shovels.

These small whales are found all over the world. However, porpoises prefer shallow waters near the shore, whereas oceanic dolphins usually stay in the deep, open seas. River dolphins live in bodies of fresh water such as the Amazon River in South America and the Yangtze River in China.

The Friendly Dolphin

Dolphins seem friendly because they always look as if they're smiling. But they aren't smiling any more than a crocodile is—that's just the way their mouths are shaped. Because of their smiling faces and playful behavior, people often have the feeling that dolphins are almost human. And in many ways they are!

Dolphins live in pods of about twenty to one hundred members. They are very social animals. That means they live together like a close family, helping one another when they become sick or hurt. If an injured dolphin cannot swim, others will hold it up to the water's surface so it can breathe.

Dolphins also play together. They chase one another endlessly, as if they are playing tag. A group of them will suddenly leap out of the water. Then they will race away from one another as soon as they splash back down.

When dolphins hunt, they work together as a team. For example, they will spread out and form a circle, or "dolphin net," around a school of fish. Then, taking turns, a few dolphins dart into the school and eat while the rest herd the fish.

Dr. Kenneth Norris of the University of California at Santa Cruz has been studying dolphin echolocation for more than 45 years. The dolphin family has the most sensitive echolocation system of all the whales. Their echolocation is so good that they can find a vitamin pill in an aquarium tank. Dr. Norris believes that dolphins and other toothed whales also use their sound waves to stun their food. He has watched bottlenose dolphins and killer whales chasing schools of fish. After a while, the fish begin to slow down and wander in every direction. The whales stun the fish with sound waves so that they are easy to catch.

Like any large family, dolphin pods have certain rules about the behavior of their members. Dr. Norris noticed that dolphins in tanks turn off their echolocation when they come up behind another dolphin. He realized that they don't want to stun other dolphins with their sound sprays. He also saw that dolphins rarely face each other. This is because their sound sprays shoot straight out from the front of their heads!

For this reason, dolphins in a pod always swim side by side. The smallest head movement of one dolphin causes the entire pod to move in the same direction. Each dolphin pays attention to the signals of every other dolphin in the pod. This is how the pod steers itself.

If one dolphin behaves very badly, the rest of the

pod has nothing to do with it. Most dolphins cannot bear to be separated from the pod. Some may even die of loneliness. But as soon as dolphins are reunited with their pods, they perk up.

Dolphins seem to form strong friendships with humans as well as with other dolphins. Many stories have been told about these friendships. The story of Opo, a female bottlenose dolphin, is especially touching.

One day early in 1955, Opo appeared at Opononi Beach in New Zealand and began frolicking with swimmers. She loved playing with the children, tossing balls and giving them rides on her back. If any child played too roughly, Opo would swim away and slap her tail on the water in protest. She never hurt the children, no matter what they did to her.

Opo's fame spread, and people came from miles around to see her. About a year after Opo's arrival, she was found stranded on the beach. Heartbroken, the townspeople buried her in a marked grave covered with flowers.

Studying Dolphins

When you visit an aquarium, you can see dolphins performing many tricks. They have been trained to ring bells, toss Frisbees, jump through hoops, and walk across the water on their tails. They can even play basketball, leaping out of the water to "dunk" a shot through a hoop.

The first dolphin to be trained was Flippy. Flippy lived in Marineland, an aquarium in Florida. In

1950, Marineland asked Adolph Frohn, a Ringling Brothers Circus trainer, to teach Flippy tricks. Frohn decided to teach Flippy to jump through a hoop. He knew that the secret to training any kind of animal was teaching tricks one step at a time.

First Frohn placed a net in the water and stood on one side of it with a piece of fish. Flippy was on the other side of the net. Frohn then called, "Jump, Flippy!" For a while, Flippy just swam around, looking at the fish. Finally he jumped over the net. As soon as he did, Frohn gave him the fish, patted him, and told him, "Good boy, Flippy!"

Then Frohn replaced the net with a rope. Each time Flippy jumped over it, his trainer gave him a reward and praised him. Frohn kept raising the rope. Soon Flippy was jumping 10 feet into the air. Finally Frohn took away the rope and held up a hoop. Flippy didn't want to go through such a small hole. But he trusted his trainer, and pretty soon he jumped through it. Adolf Frohn taught Flippy his first trick! But Flippy also taught Adolf Frohn a lot about dolphins. Here's what Adolf Frohn learned.

A dolphin has to like you before it will do something for you—and you must never try to force a dolphin to do anything. It will stop eating and die rather than do something it doesn't want to do. Dolphins won't work if they're bored, so tricks must be challenging to keep them interested. Dolphins also want more than just a fish reward. A hug and some praise tell them that they're appreciated.

One of the reasons dolphins can be taught so many different tricks is that they love to play. It's also possible that dolphins learn tricks in order to spend time with the trainer. Some researchers think dolphins learn tricks because they find life in the aquariums boring. Others, however, believe that dolphins simply enjoy learning. This ability to learn makes humans wonder just how intelligent dolphins really are.

Brainy Students

Dolphins have large brains compared with the size of their bodies. That means they are intelligent creatures. They can learn to do things much more quickly than other animals. They are able to learn a trick just by watching other dolphins do it. They also seem to have no trouble remembering the tricks they've been taught. A dolphin named Paddy was taught to pick out different shapes. This is a difficult task for most animals, but Paddy had no trouble learning it. The trainers then waited 7 months before asking Paddy to do the trick again. Right away, Paddy chose the right shapes.

This ability to learn tricks and remember them means that dolphins are intelligent. But can dolphins figure out the reasons for things the way humans can? One trainer taught dolphins to remove trash from their aquarium. Each time a dolphin brought a piece of trash to the trainer, it got a fish. But one dolphin named Mr. Spock always seemed to bring back more trash than the others did.

The trainer discovered that Mr. Spock had hidden away a whole pile of trash. He had collected it before cleanup time and saved it. At cleaning time, he then cashed in his trash for fish. No one taught Mr. Spock to store trash in order to get rewards later. He figured it out all by himself!

Dolphin Talk

For years scientists have listened to the sounds that dolphins make. Today they are using computers to figure out what these sounds mean. It is believed that there are three kinds of sounds. For echolocation, dolphins use clicks and mews. They bark, cluck, yelp, squeak, and squawk when they are upset, afraid, or angry.

Dolphins also whistle when they want to identify themselves. Each dolphin has a special whistle. This sound is a *call note*. When a dolphin uses its call note in one way, it says, "My name is Allie. I'm over here." The call can be used in a different way to say, "Help! Allie is in trouble!" As soon as other dolphins hear that call, they rush to help. Certain whistles have other meanings, too. One kind of whistle says, "Hey! Here's something new!" Another kind means "Danger!" Another says, "Food!"

Dolphins also use their call note when they are herding schools of fish for feeding. Calling out in this way tells the group exactly where each dolphin is. They can then make sure that there is just enough space between them to form a net around the fish.

Dr. Louis Herman is a psychology professor and the director of the Kewalo Basin Marine Mammal Laboratory in Hawaii. For more than 10 years, he has been working there with two bottlenose dolphins named Phoenix and Akeakamai, or Ake. Dr. Herman is teaching each of these dolphins a different kind of language. Phoenix is learning a language made up of computer whistles. Ake's language is based on hand signals and whistles.

Dr. Herman has proved that dolphins understand the meaning of words. They can even understand three-word sentences. But most important, they understand how the order of words changes the meaning of a sentence. For example, the two dolphins can tell the difference between these two sentences: "Hoop, fetch, ball" means "Find the *hoop* and carry it to the *ball*" and "Ball, fetch, hoop" means "Find the *ball* and carry it to the *hoop*."

Scientists aren't sure how much dolphins can understand. But they all agree that dolphins communicate with one another by using sounds and body language. One dolphin often "talks" while the rest are quiet. Then another one "speaks" while the others seem to listen.

At the Dolphin Research Center in Grassy Key, Florida, six dolphins are helping to teach humans. The dolphins' students are mentally handicapped children. The dolphins are given pictures with simple words written on them. They take the pictures to the children. If a child says the word on the picture correctly, he or she gets a ride on the dolphin. Researchers at the center say this program is working! The dolphins seem to know that the children are more helpless than other people, so they treat them very gently. And the children are learning 10 times more quickly with the dolphins than they do in classrooms!

You and the Whales

Whales have helped us for hundreds of years. Now they need our help. You can avoid buying things made of plastic or packaged in Styrofoam. These things might get dumped into the ocean and harm sea animals. You can also buy tuna that has a "dolphin-free" label on it. You can even ask your grocer to put only "dolphin-free" tuna on the grocery shelf.

Your family or your class at school might want to adopt a humpback whale through the Whale Adoption Project. For information, write to: The International Wildlife Coalition, 634 Falmouth Highway, P.O. Box 388, North Falmouth, Massachusetts 02556-0388.

Whale Watching

You can see small whales like dolphins and belugas at these aquariums:

Baltimore Aquarium, Baltimore, MD

Miami Seaquarium, Miami, FL

Mystic Marinelife Aquarium, Mystic, CT

New York Aquarium, Brooklyn, NY

Seaworld, Orlando, FL

Seaworld, San Antonio, TX

Seaworld, San Diego, CA

If you happen to live near an ocean, you can take a trip on a whale-watching boat. In the northeastern states you can see blue, fin, minke, beluga, and pilot whales. You can also watch harbor porpoises and many different kinds of dolphins. Along the West Coast you can watch gray, blue, fin, sperm, hump-back, and pilot whales, as well as many different kinds of dolphins and porpoises. Dolphins frolic all year long in Florida, and many humpbacks spend the winter in Hawaii.

Other titles in the Explorer Books series

BATS

DISASTERS

GREAT APES

MUMMIES

POISONOUS CREATURES

SECRET CODES

SHARKS

WOLVES